Spooky

JOKES

SPOOKY JOKES

An Hachette UK Company
www.hachette.co.uk

Summersdale Publishers Ltd
Part of Octopus Publishing Group Limited
Carmelite House
50 Victoria Embankment
LONDON
EC4Y 0DZ
UK

www.summersdale.com

Printed and bound in China

ISBN: 978-1-78783-591-7

Substantial discounts on bulk quantities of Summersdale books are available to corporations, professional associations and other organizations. For details contact general enquiries: telephone: +44 (0) 1243 771107 or email: enquiries@summersdale.com.

Spooky

JOKES

ROBIN GRAVES

summersdale

What is a spook's favourite plant?

Bam-BOO!

What do you call a snoozing werewolf?

An unaware-wolf.

Where does a ghost go to let his hair down at weekends?

Anywhere he can boo-gie.

Why are skeletons so calm?

Because nothing gets under their skin.

What did the little bat learn
on her first day at school?

The alpha-bat.

What do geeky spiders
like doing?

Making websites.

Wanda the witch had always wanted
to be a model but her dad insisted
she study potions instead.

Graduating with honours, she pleaded
to be allowed to take part in a fashion
show, so that she might, just once,
experience the thrill of the catwalk.

Her dad finally agreed, and Wanda was a hit.

"I was wrong," her dad said. "You go
get yourself an agent. After all,
if you've got it, haunt it."

What is a werewolf's favourite day of the week?

Moonday.

Who presided over the spooks' Halloween party?

The ghostess with the mostest.

**Who did Frankenstein invite
to his Halloween party?**

Anyone he could dig up.

**Which section of the newspaper
does a monster read first?**

The horror-scopes.

A wizard walks into a Halloween party shop and sees a cute little rat sitting on a banshee's shoulder.

He asks the banshee, "Does your rat bite?" The banshee replies, "No, my rat doesn't bite."

The wizard reaches out to pat the rat, but the rodent promptly gives him a sharp nip.

"Ouch!" he cries. "I thought you said your rat doesn't bite!"

The banshee gives him a pitying look and replies, "It doesn't. But that isn't my rat!"

What's a monster's favourite bean?

A human bean.

What's problematic about twin witches?

You never know which witch is which.

When do werewolves like
to go trick or treating?

Howl-o-ween.

How many vampires
are in this room?

**I don't know, I can't
Count Draculas.**

Where do baby ghosts go while their parents are at work?

Dayscare.

Knock, knock!

Who's there?

Cereal!

Cereal who?

Cereal killer – bet you've been *dying* to meet me!

**What's a mummy's
favorite flower?**

Chrysanthamummies.

**What do you call a
bat in a belfry?**

A dingbat.

Two zombies went to a Halloween party.

One said to the other, "A lady just rolled her eyes at me. What should I do?"

The other zombie replied, "Don't be rude, roll them back to her!"

What do you call an undercover spider?

A spy-der.

Why are vampires similar to false teeth?

They all come out at night.

How do witches fix their hair?

With scare spray.

Why don't monsters
get carried away?

Because they creep it real.

A hungry zombie was walking through the woods looking for something to eat when it spied two men. One was sitting on a tree trunk reading a book, the other was typing away on his laptop. The zombie quickly pounced on the man reading and gobbled him up. Relieved, but curious, the other man asked why the zombie had picked his friend and not him. "Ah, but that's easy," said the zombie. "Even a brain-dead zombie like me knows that readers digest and writers cramp."

Why do demons and ghouls like each other so much?

No idea, but demons are a ghoul's best friend.

What kind of music do mummies like best?

Wrap.

**How do you make a
skeleton laugh?**

It's easy – just tickle
his funny bone.

Why did the corpse get upset?

It made a grave error!

Two swamp monsters swim
into a concrete wall.

One turns to the other
and says, "Dam!"

What's a little monster's
favourite storybook?

Scary Poppins.

Did you hear about the
zombie who ate superglue?

His lips were sealed.

What do little vampires
like to play at school?

Bat's cradle.

A revered archaeologist was convinced he had found the site of an ancient Egyptian tomb.

While digging, he was wildly excited to uncover a highly unusual mummified body that was covered in chocolate and nuts.

The newspaper headlines the following day read: "Lost Egyptian royalty found! Experts believe it may be Pharaoh Rocher."

**What musical instrument
do skeletons excel at?**

The trom-bone.

**How do bats fly without
bumping into anything?**

They use their wing mirrors.

**How do you know a
corpse is angry?**

They flip their lid!

**Two fire-breathing demons
were kayaking when they felt
chilly. Using their natural talents,
they lit a fire in the vessel.**

Unsurprisingly it sank,
proving that you can't have
your kayak and heat it too.

The manager of the haunted hotel wanted to buy something to give trick or treaters on Halloween, and so, leaving his deputy in charge, he set off to buy something special that would really impress the kids.

On his return he proudly showed off a big bag of candy canes, which he explained he had managed to buy really cheaply.

"Wow!" said his deputy, "you would never know that they came from the bargain basement, they look great!"

"I know," acknowledged his manager. "They're in mint condition."

**What would happen if
tarantulas were as big as horses?**

If one bit you, you could
ride it to hospital!

**Why did the corpse
like Halloween?**

He always won the
best-dressed prize.

Why didn't the skeleton go
to see the scary movie?

They didn't have the guts.

What type of Halloween
candy is never on time?

ChocoLATE.

**What did the vampire say
when his girlfriend left him?**

"Fangs for the memories."

And what did she reply?

"So long, sucker."

Knock, knock!

Who's there?

Eva!

Eva who?

Eva you're deaf or your doorbell isn't working – TRICK OR TREAT!

What kind of key does a ghost use?

A spoo-key.

Two vampires were comparing
their favourite newspapers.

One liked a popular tabloid because of the
celebrity column. The other preferred one that
had the latest stock market information.

While they tried to convince each other
that their favourite paper was best, a
third vampire joined in the conversation.

When asked what his preference was,
the newcomer answered, "I just like
whichever has the best circulation."

Why did the ghost visit the bar?

They wanted some boos.

How do you use an ancient
Egyptian doorbell?

Toot and come in!

Why don't witches ride their brooms when they are angry?

They're worried about flying off the handle.

Why didn't the skeleton go to the party?

He had no body to go with.

In the graveyard, one dark and stormy night,
a ghost had an argument with a bone.
"Oi!" he shouted at the bone, I
want a word with you. At least I
think I do, are you the tibia?
The bone looked aghast and replied: "Tibia
or not tibia? That is the question."

Did you see the horror movie about a crazed killer who was dressed in red?

It was called *Santa's Slay*.

Corpse jokes should carry a health warning.

They can make you split your sides.

**The cemetery up the
hill is really popular.**

People are dying to get in!

Why did Dracula's fangs fall out?

Because he candy-flossed.

**Why did the spider move
into the haunted house?**

Because ghosts can't
break their webs.

**What's the best way
to hold a bat?**

By the handle.

What do you call an
idiotic skeleton?

Bonehead.

Why was the mummy
feeling so tense?

**Because they were
all wound up.**

Knock, knock!

Who's there?

A vampire!

A vampire who?

Look, just a vampire, OK? I'm really sorry.
I did try my absolute hardest to
come up with something as a funny
punchline, but vampires are no good at
Halloween humour - we just suck.

What did the spider say to her husband when he tried to explain why he was late?

You're spinning me a yarn.

What should you never say to the Grim Reaper?

"Over my dead body!"

What was the movie about a green ogre on Halloween called?

Shriek.

Why was Cinderella so bad at football?

Because her coach was a pumpkin.

Three vampires walked into a bar.
"And what would you gentleman
like?" asked the waiter.

The first vampire said,
"I'll have a pint of blood."

The second said, "I'll have the same."

The third vampire asked
for a glass of plasma.

The waiter nodded and called
to the bartender, "That's two
bloods and a blood light."

Knock, knock!

Who's there?

Gladys!

Gladys who!

Gladys my last Halloween knock-knock joke!

What do you call a goblin with a broken leg?

A hoblin.

Why do ghouls go on diets?

So they can keep their
ghoulish figures.

What do you call a
witch's garage?

A broom closet.

**Why are werewolves
better than vampires?**

Werewolves don't have a
problem with steaks.

**What are jack-o'-
lanterns afraid of?**

Things that go pumpkin
the night.

**What do barflies say
on Halloween?**

"Trick or tequila."

**Why did the headless
horseman go into business?**

He wanted to get a-head.

A ghoul decided to host a lavish party for all the monsters and spooks in the neighbourhood.

Anxious to show off his elegant home, he called in the finest interior designers and party planners and hired the most exclusive caterers and entertainers.

When the big night came, he noticed that one room was entirely empty.

The lavish buffet was untouched, the champagne stood unpopped and the sumptuous couches were unsat upon.

"Why aren't you partying in here?" he demanded of a passing zombie.

How dare you!" exclaimed the zombie. "As if the undead would party in the living room!"

What do you call a particularly pretty pumpkin?

Gourdgeous!

What do you call a witch at the beach?

A sand-witch.

Patient: I keep seeing a vampire with sharp teeth.

Doctor: Have you seen a psychiatrist?

Patient: No, just the vampire.

What is a ghost's favourite meal?

Spooketti Bolognese.

A man was walking through the graveyard late one night. Suddenly he heard a strange clattering noise and a skeleton ran past him before disappearing from view. Terrified, but intrigued, he picked up his pace and followed in the skeleton's footsteps. Turning the corner, he watched in amazement as the spook began climbing a tree, not resting until it had reached a high branch. Looking down and spotting the man, the skeleton called out, "Well, wouldn't you run if you were nothing but bones and a dog was chasing you?"

**What do you get if you cross
a tarantula with a lily?**

I'm not sure, but I wouldn't
try smelling it!

**What candy did the stand-up
comic give to trick or treaters?**

Snickers.

**Why did the ghost walk
into a bar but have to leave
almost immediately?**

The bartender said it
was company policy
not to serve spirits.

How do vampires travel?

On blood vessels.

Knock, knock!

Who's there?

Armageddon!

Armageddon who?

It's too spooky – Armageddon
out of here!

Did you hear about the spirit
who refused painkillers during
a root canal procedure?

**They wanted to transcend
dental medication.**

What is a little monster's
favourite storybook?

The Gingerdead Man.

A clairvoyant liked to walk barefoot.

Unfortunately this resulted in enormous calluses on their feet.

They also didn't eat a great deal and the lack of food made them a bit frail and caused their breath to smell pretty bad.

All in all, they were... a super calloused fragile mystic hexed by halitosis.

What did the waiter say to the skeleton?

"Bone appétit!"

What do you get if you cross a werewolf and a pet dog?

A traumatized postman.

**Why wouldn't the witch
wear a flat hat?**

They didn't see the point.

**What is a ghoul's
favourite game?**

Hide and shriek.

A little boy was out trick or treating on Halloween when he saw a witch mounting her broomstick.

Scared but fascinated, he watched her zoom up and down the street.

Finally plucking up the courage to speak to her, he asked, "What are you doing on that?"

Looking down her warty nose at the youngster, the witch replied, "My sister's got the vacuum cleaner."

What do you get if you drop a pumpkin?

Squash.

What do you call a spook doing the vacuuming?

The Grim Sweeper.

Why are haunted houses so tall?

**Because they have so
many horror stories.**

What did the jack-o'-lantern
say to his date when they
realized they were being
watched by their friends?

**"Let's give 'em pumpkin
to talk about."**

What is the most-played song at the spooks' Halloween party?

"Ghouls Just Wanna Have Fun".

What do you call a werewolf that can't decide on an outfit?

A what-to-wear-wolf.

How do you know when a vampire has been tampering with the goods in a bakery?

The doughnuts have had their centres sucked out.

What is a ghost's favourite dessert?

I-scream!

A photographer is determined to capture a ghost on film and goes to a haunted castle on Halloween.

Sure enough, a ghost appears. Better still, he is a friendly spook and gladly poses for pictures.

The photographer is ecstatic and makes haste to his studio to develop the images.

Tragically, he finds that all his pictures are underexposed, not even a whiff of his friendly ghost.

Which only goes to prove that sometimes the spirit is willing, but the flash is weak...

I opened my door on Halloween
and got slapped by a spider.

There's a nasty bug
going around.

How do you make a witch itch?

Take away their "W".

What is a vampire's
favourite fruit?

A necktarine.

What does a hungry zombie
call a sheep that has been
dipped in chocolate and
coated with sprinkles?

A candy baa.

A law enforcement officer was in the butcher's shop buying steak for their dinner. Without warning they shouted "FREEZE!" and proceeded to slap their cuffs on a werewolf that was lurking by the counter.

The butcher turned to the officer in amazement and asked, "What are you doing; why are you arresting one of my best customers?!"

"I'm sorry," replied the law enforcement officer, "but they were chop lifting."

Knock, knock!

Who's there?

Europe!

Europe who?

Europe'ning the door too slow – hurry up with the Halloween candy!

Where does a ghost like to visit?

Mali-boo.

Why did the girl dump her vampire boyfriend?

She found him a real
pain in the neck.

What is a spook's favourite Shakespeare play?

Romeo and Ghouliet.

**Today I shocked the postal
worker by opening the door
wearing a horror mask.**

I don't know what shocked
them most, the mask or that
I know where they live!

**What do you call a
chubby pumpkin?**

A plump-kin.

What would you find
in a ghost's nose?

Boo-gers.

What did the mummy movie
director say when the final
scene had been shot?

It's a wrap.

The priest was very upset they lost their favourite Bible while on a pilgrimage.

A month later, a bat flew into their church, carrying the Bible in its mouth.

The priest was astounded. They took the book out of the creature's mouth, fell to their knees and exclaimed, "It's a miracle!"

"Not really," said the bat. "Your name and address is written inside the cover."

What did one bat say to another?

Let's hang out together.

If a monster has twenty Halloween chocolate bars and eats all but one, what does he have?

Room to gobble you up!

Knock, knock!

Who's there?

Chicken!

Chicken who?

**Chicken your cauldron;
I can smell burning!**

**What subject do witches
do best at in school?**

Spelling.

A ghost had been to the funfair with his friends.

"Did you have a good time?" his wife enquired on his return.

"Yes, I did," replied her spooky spouse. "I went on the scary-go-round and the roller-ghoster.

"I wasn't going to, but then I thought why not? You've got to live a little."

**What do mummies do
on their holidays?**

Unwind.

**What do you get if you cross a
bat with a lonely hearts club?**

A lot of blind dates.

What did the spider say
when he tore his new web?

Darn it!

What is the best thing
about Halloween candy?

**It's half price in the
sale the day after!**

What is it called when two corpses reach the finishing line at the same time?

A dead heat!

What do you call a spider with twenty eyes?

A spiiiiiiiiiiiiiiiiiiiiider.

What dessert is served at the haunted house?

Boo-berry pie.

Did you hear about the werewolf who won the talent show?

He was a howling success.

Two zombies are each carrying
a brace of dead raccoons.

Attempting to board an airplane,
the flight attendant stops them at the
door and says, "I'm sorry, gentlemen, but
it's only one carrion per passenger."

What did one pumpkin say
to the other when they
met on the doorstep?

"Oh my gourd!"

What do you get if you cross
a vampire and a snowman?

Frostbite.

What do skeletons order in a Chinese restaurant?

Spare ribs.

What do spectators eat at the haunted Wimbledon tournament?

Strawberries and scream.

A daddy bat teaches his three children
how to suck blood and sends them
away to test their abilities.

The first child returns with a face full of blood
and says, "Dad, do you see that cow?"

"Yes I do, son."

"I sucked all of its blood!" the first one replies.

The second one comes later with
even more blood on his face and says,
"Dad, do you see that horse?"

"Yes, son."

"I sucked all of its blood!"

Finally, the third one returns with
even more blood on his face and says,
"Dad, do you see that wall?"

His father nods.

"I didn't."

Why is Halloween candy like a British summer?

Neither lasts very long.

Knock, knock!

Who's there?

Voodoo!

Voodoo who?

Voodoo you think you are!

What do you call two young married spiders?

Newly webs!

What was the first thing the werewolf ate after getting his teeth cleaned?

The dentist.

How do you mend a broken
jack-o'-lantern?

With a pumpkin patch.

What do bats do at night?

Aerobatics.

Victor the vampire was having trouble with the land adjacent to his property.

It was a grave problem.

How did the skeleton prepare for his exams?

He boned up on all the facts.

The teacher of Spooky Cookery addressed her class, "Put up your hand if you know what the five major monster food groups are."

The students thought hard, but only Frank put up his hand. "I know, Miss! The five monster food groups are chocolate, gum, candy, cake and beans."

"Beans?" queried the teacher. "Yes," said Frank. "Human beans!"

What happened to the werewolf who swallowed a wristwatch?

He got ticks.

Why did the vampire need mouthwash?

To deal with his bat breath.

**What kind of emails does
Count Dracula receive?**

Fang mail.

**Why did Frankenstein hold his
ghost friends above his head?**

He wanted to lift his spirits.

A man was out walking one day when he felt something crunch beneath his sandal.

On inspection, he saw that he had accidently trodden on a large spider, killing it outright.

Mortified that he had killed a living creature, he sat down on the grass.

Soon, his friend came along and the man told him what had happened.

"I feel so bad that I stepped on the poor little beast. You should have seen him; he looked genuinely crushed."

**Did you hear about the
werewolves who met for lunch?**

They wolfed it down.

**Why is a skeleton like a
weather forecaster?**

He always knows when the
weather will change because
he can feel it in his bones.

Where do ghosts like
to trick or treat?

Dead ends.

When is it bad luck to be
followed by a black cat?

When you're a mouse.

What is a vampire's least favourite food?

Steak.

What do you call a hairy howler who lives next door to a dam?

A weir-wolf.

Knock, knock!

Who's there?

Justin!

Justin who?

Justin time for Halloween!

**Why are ghosts such
useless liars?**

You can see right
through them.

Bill and Mike were walking home after a Halloween party and decided to take a shortcut through the graveyard.

Suddenly startled by a tap-tap-tap noise coming from the shadows, they clutched each other in terror. About to scream, they spotted an old man chiselling away at a headstone.

"Wowzer!" Bill exclaimed, as he and Mike breathed a collective sigh of relief. "You scared the living daylights out of us – we thought you were a ghost! Why are you working at this hour?"

"Those idiot kids of mine!" the old man grumbled. "They misspelled my name!"

If you're interested in finding out more about our books, find us on Facebook at **Summersdale Publishers** and follow us on Twitter at **@Summersdale**.

www.summersdale.com